FAMINE AND DUST

DUST BOWL

45th Parallel Press

Published in the United States of America by Cherry Lake Publishing
Ann Arbor, Michigan
www.cherrylakepublishing.com

Reading Adviser: Marla Conn MS, Ed., Literacy specialist, Read-Ability, Inc.
Book Designer: Felicia Macheske

Photo Credits: © Pinkyone/Shutterstock.com, cover, 1; Dorothea Lange, Library of Congress, LC-DIG-fsa-8b32396, 5; LC-DIG-ppmsca-23845, 11; LC-USF34-016109-E, 21; LC-DIG-fsa-8b27245, 23; LC-DIG-fsa-8b34383, 25; LC-USF34-016264-C, 29; D. L. Kernodle, Library of Congress, LC-USF34-001615-ZE, 6; Arthur Rothstein, Library of Congress, LC-USF34-004106-E, 12; © Earl D. Walker/Shutterstock.com, 17; © Everett Historical/Shutterstock.com, 18

Graphic Elements Throughout: © Chipmunk131/Shutterstock.com; © Nowik Sylwia/Shutterstock.com; © Andrey_Popov/Shutterstock.com; © NadzeyaShanchuk/Shutterstock.com; © KathyGold/Shutterstock.com; © Black creator/Shutterstock.com; © Edvard Molnar/Shutterstock.com; © Elenadesign/Shutterstock.com; © estherpoon/Shutterstock.com

45th Parallel Press is an imprint of Cherry Lake Publishing.

Library of Congress Cataloging-in-Publication Data has been filed and is available at catalog.loc.gov

Cherry Lake Publishing would like to acknowledge the work of The Partnership for 21st Century Skills. Please visit www.p21.org for more information.

Printed in the United States of America
Corporate Graphics

A Note on Dramatic Retellings

Participating in Readers Theater, or dramatic retellings, can greatly improve reading skills, especially fluency. The books in the **BEHIND THE CURTAIN** series give readers opportunities to learn about important historical events in a fun and engaging way. These books serve as a bridge to more complex texts. All the characters are real figures from history; however, their stories have been fictionalized. To learn more about the people and the events, check out the Viewpoints and Perspectives series and the Perspectives Library series, as the **BEHIND THE CURTAIN** books are aligned to these stories.

TABLE of CONTENTS

HiSTORICAL BACKGROUND

The Dust Bowl took place in the 1930s. It took place in areas around the Great Plains. This included Kansas, Colorado, Oklahoma, Texas, and New Mexico. States around them were impacted too. Big dust storms covered the land. People couldn't breathe. Some people and animals choked to death. Houses were buried. Really big dust storms were called "black blizzards." People couldn't see. They couldn't move.

The worst dust storm was called Black Sunday. It took place on Sunday, April 14, 1935. Winds traveled at high speeds. Dust storms took over cities. Dust darkened the skies.

Living in the Dust Bowl was hard. People had to move. Many migrated to California. There were jobs in California. Poor farmers who migrated were called Okies.

FLASH FACT!

Many people built farms on the Great Plains in the early 1900s.

Vocabulary

Great Plains (GRAYT PLAYNZ) area of flat land in the middle of the United States

blizzard (BLIZ-urd) a really bad snowstorm with high winds

migrated (MYE-grate-id) moved from one area to another

FLASH FACT!

Dust storms billowed over the plains. Some rose up to 10,000 feet high.

Vocabulary

severe (suh-VEER) very difficult or harsh

drought (DROUT) a long period of no rain, dry season

starved (STAHRVD) suffered from lack of food

graze (GRAZE) to eat grass in a field

cattle (KAT-uhl) a group of cows

environment (en-VYE-ruhn-muhnt) natural world

The Dust Bowl was caused by several things. First, there was a severe drought. This drought lasted 10 years. The soil became dry. It turned to dust. The land became a desert. Farmers could no longer grow crops. People starved. Second, farmers plowed the land to grow wheat or to graze cattle. Wheat doesn't hold the soil. The land was treated badly. This destroyed the grass and soil. Farmers had changed the environment. The land started to blow away.

The government helped. Programs were created to help farmers. Programs were created to give people jobs. Rain came in 1939. This ended the drought. About 2.5 million people migrated. About 7,000 people died.

CAST of CHARACTERS

NARRATOR: person who helps tell the story

EVELYN BROWN: migrant in California who came from Kansas, daughter of **hardware** store owners

LEONA ELLSAESSER: young girl who lived through Black Sunday, daughter of a cattle dealer from Kansas

VERNON THOMPSON: farmer from Oklahoma who stayed there during the Dust Bowl

HARVEY PICKREL: farmer from York, Nebraska

DOROTHEA LANGE: famous **photographer** who works for the government

FLORENCE LEE: photographer from California who works for the government

BACKSTORY
SPOTLIGHT BIOGRAPHY

Florence Owens Thompson is known as "Migrant Mother." She's the subject of Dorothea Lange's most famous photograph. Thompson's face captured the worry and despair of the Dust Bowl. Thompson was born on September 1, 1903. She was born in Oklahoma. Both her parents were Cherokee. She was 32 years old when the photo was taken. She was in Nipomo, California, at that time. She was heading to Shafter, California. She was poor. She had seven children. She had just sold her car tires to buy food. She said, "I worked in hospitals. I tended bar. I cooked. I worked in the fields. I done a little bit of everything to make a living for my kids." She died on September 16, 1983. Her gravestone reads, "Florence Leona Thompson, Migrant Mother — A Legend of the Strength of American Motherhood."

Vocabulary
migrant (MYE-gruhnt) a person who moves from one place to another

hardware (HAHRD-wair) tools and machines

photographer (fuh-TAH-gruh-fur) someone who takes pictures with a camera, especially as a job

FLASH FACT!
The Dust Bowl affected over 1 million acres (404,686 hectares) of land.

ACT 1

NARRATOR: *It's late April in 1935. "Black Sunday" recently happened.* **LEONA ELLSAESSER** *and* **EVELYN BROWN** *are in Kansas. They're standing outside.*

EVELYN: Why aren't you wearing your mask? We should go inside.

LEONA: Just one more minute. I want to get as much sun as I can. After Black Sunday, I'll never take the sun for granted.

EVELYN: That day was really bad. It was the worst dust storm we've had.

LEONA: We were stuck in the house for days. We shut the doors and windows. But the dust still got in. It even got into our noses and eyes.

EVELYN: Same here. We felt like **prisoners**.

LEONA: Some of my friends got really sick.

EVELYN: Dust can clog up our lungs. People have died from it.

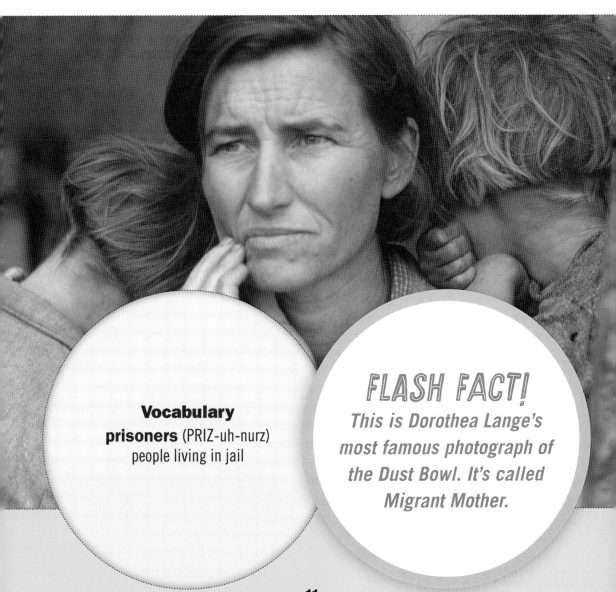

Vocabulary
prisoners (PRIZ-uh-nurz)
people living in jail

FLASH FACT!
This is Dorothea Lange's most famous photograph of the Dust Bowl. It's called Migrant Mother.

LEONA: Not just people. Some of Daddy's cattle are dying as well. But the worst is the darkness. I can't wait for these black blizzards to stop.

EVELYN: For me, the worst is the high winds. The winds blow so fast. They sound like they're screaming.

LEONA: Speaking of winds, I feel a chill in the air.

EVELYN: The winds are picking up again.

LEONA: The sky is getting dark. It's time to go!

NARRATOR: *It's May in 1935.* **VERNON THOMPSON** *and* **HARVEY PICKREL** *are at a meeting. Farmers meet to discuss* ***relief*** *efforts.*

VERNON: I hate taking money from the government. But I don't know what else to do.

HARVEY: This drought has lasted too long. Without rain, my crops have failed. Without crops, nothing holds the soil in place. My farm has become a dust cloud.

Vocabulary
relief (rih-LEEF) release from pain or distress

FLASH FACT!
Farmers tried to save their crops.

VERNON: These black blizzards! They're worse than **tornadoes**! They're ruining everything. Every morning, I find more and more animal **corpses**. My farm is like a **graveyard**. Our sheep and cattle are dying.

HARVEY: I can't wait for the "**Dirty Thirties**" to pass. We need rain.

VERNON: We also need to learn how to farm better. These government **experts** are saying that we worked the lands too much. We didn't give the lands a rest. That's why the soil dried up. We also need to plant more trees. Trees slow down the winds.

HARVEY: Even ships in the Atlantic Ocean are covered in our dust.

VERNON: Dust is flying from all over the place. I can tell where dust is coming from by the color. Red is Oklahoma dirt. Black is from Kansas. Gray is from Colorado and New Mexico.

HARVEY: We're all in this together. We made this mess. And now we have to fix it. I'll do whatever it takes to heal and keep my land.

LOCATION SHOOTING
REAL-WORLD SETTING

U.S. Route 66 had several names. One is the Will Rogers Highway. Another is Main Street of America. Another is the Mother Road. Route 66 was one of the first U.S. highways. It was built in 1926. It was the first highway to be paved. This happened in 1938. It ran from Chicago, Illinois, to Santa Monica, California. It crossed Missouri, Kansas, Oklahoma, Texas, New Mexico, and Arizona. It covered 2,448 miles (3,940 kilometers). It was mainly flat. It was the main road for Dust Bowl migrants. Small towns grew along the road. People set up businesses. They set up gas stations. They set up restaurants. Some parts were dangerous. These parts were called "bloody 66." There were dangerous turns. Route 66 was replaced in 1985. It was replaced by the Interstate Highway System.

Vocabulary

tornadoes (tor-NAY-dohz) storm winds that spin

corpses (KORPS-iz) dead bodies

graveyard (GRAVE-yahrd) a place where dead bodies are buried

Dirty Thirties (DUR-tee THUR-teez) name for the 1930s

experts (EK-spurts) people who have a lot of knowledge

FLASH FACT!
Too much plowing is part of what caused the Dust Bowl.

EVELYN: There's not much left. I haven't ordered any new **supplies**. Business has been slow. Nobody has money to buy anything.

VERNON: I can't afford to buy new things anyway. I was hoping you'd have some used supplies.

EVELYN: I'll give you a good deal. My family and I are closing the store. We're heading to California. We hear there are jobs there.

VERNON: I thought about leaving. I feel like I'm living in a fog of dust. No matter how much I clean, dust is everywhere. I spit dust. I swallow dust. I can't stand it.

EVELYN: Being dusty is the least of my problems. It's been hard finding food.

VERNON: I've gone to bed hungry many nights. I'm a farmer. I should be able to grow food.

Vocabulary
supplies (suh-PLYEZ) materials
needed to do something

FLASH FACT!
The summer of 1936
was the hottest and
driest summer.

EVELYN: It's hard to buy food as well. There's so little food to go around.

VERNON: I should **escape** with you. My neighbors have left already.

EVELYN: Why don't you? A lot of people are leaving. Life is too hard here. The drought doesn't seem to be ending.

VERNON: How can I leave? I love it here. I love my farm. I've lived here my whole life. Plus, I'm too poor to leave.

EVELYN: We're too poor to stay.

VERNON: I have to make it work. I started growing turnips and potatoes. I grow enough to eat. I grow a little to sell. I grow some to hold down the soil.

EVELYN: Hopefully, it works out for you. I wish you the best of luck.

Vocabulary
escape (ih-SKAPE) to get away

FLASH FACT!
One black blizzard traveled 2,000 miles (3,219 km) to the East Coast on May 11, 1934.

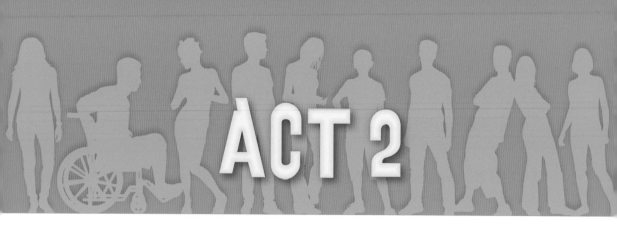

ACT 2

NARRATOR: *It's early summer in 1935.* **LEONA ELLSAESSER** *is visiting* **EVELYN BROWN**.

LEONA: It looks like you're almost **packed**.

EVELYN: My parents aren't young anymore. I'm worried about how they'll do on this trip. It's not an easy trip.

LEONA: You'll be traveling with a lot of other people. Just stay on Route 66. It'll take you all the way to California.

EVELYN: I'll miss you! I'll probably never see you again. Are you sure you and your family don't want to come with us?

LEONA: We thought about it. So many people have already left. But my parents don't think California will be any better. They've heard a lot of stories about **hardships**. They'd rather stick it out here.

EVELYN: To stay or to go? I don't know what the right choice is.

Vocabulary

packed (PAKD) loaded objects into containers in order to move

hardships (HAHRD-ships) struggles, bad times

FLASH FACT!
Many plains families moved West. They hoped for better lives.

NARRATOR: *It's late summer in 1935.* **DOROTHEA LANGE** *and* **FLORENCE LEE** *are on Route 66.*

DOROTHEA: This is the hardest job I've ever had.

FLORENCE: It's **heartbreaking**. There are so many sad stories. People are suffering in different ways.

DOROTHEA: People are also **surviving** in different ways. The human spirit is strong.

FLORENCE: Are you working for the government as well?

DOROTHEA: Yes. The government wants me to take photographs. It wants to **document** the **plight** of the Dust Bowl **victims** and migrants.

FLORENCE: This is such important work. The whole world needs to see what's happening.

DOROTHEA: I hope our photos encourage people to help.

FLORENCE: Let's hope our photos stop this from happening in the future. We need to learn from this.

Vocabulary

heartbreaking (HAHRT-brayk-ing) very sad

surviving (sur-VYE-ving) living through

document (DAHK-yuh-muhnt) to record

plight (PLITE) hard situation

victims (VIK-tuhmz) people who suffered through something bad

FLASH FACT!

The government hired photographers.

Note

NARRATOR: EVELYN BROWN *has driven many miles. Her car broke down several times. Dust had gotten into the* **engine***. But Evelyn finally arrives in California.* DOROTHEA LANGE *and* FLORENCE LEE *meet her at a migrant camp. Evelyn lets them take photos of her.*

EVELYN: Why did that man just call me an "Okie"? I'm not from Oklahoma. I'm from Kansas.

DOROTHEA: "Okie" is anyone who has moved to California due to the Dust Bowl. Some people aren't happy about all the people moving here.

FLORENCE: There are so many people. Everyone needs jobs. Farmers can pay workers almost nothing. It's not fair.

Vocabulary
engine (EN-jin) a machine that makes a car work

FLASH FACT!
All family members needed to work to make enough money.

EVELYN: We pick fruit all day long. We're working for way less than we did in Kansas.

DOROTHEA: At least you have work. Some people can't get jobs at all.

EVELYN: I do feel lucky about that. But the work is so hard. We **stoop** in the fields. We work in the hot sun.

FLORENCE: Young children carry bags twice their size. It's such a shame. Children should play, not work.

EVELYN: California isn't what I expected. The land is so **fertile**. There's so much fruit! How can people live so poorly in a rich land? We live in a **shantytown**.

FLORENCE: You're not alone. Thousands of migrants live very poorly.

EVELYN: We spent everything we had to get here. We don't have any extra money. We used our old clothes and blankets. We made a tent.

FLORENCE: I've seen many families sharing a small tent. It's awful.

EVELYN: We don't even have clean water. We use **ditch** water for cooking and washing.

BLOOPERS
HISTORICAL MISTAKES

People tried all sorts of things to make it rain. The Battle of Gettysburg was bloody. Many people died. There were 3 days of heavy fighting. Then, there was a big rain. This led some people to believe gunfire caused rain. There was a soldier in Denver, Colorado. He wanted to end a drought there. He wanted to buy lots of guns. His idea was to get people to stage fake battles. The gunfire would cause rain. Tex Thornton used the same thinking. He was from Texas. He was a bomb expert. He planned to light up rockets with dynamite. He said the rockets would hit the sky. This would cause rain. A town in Texas gave him $300. Thornton tried his idea in 1935. A dust storm came. Thornton buried his rockets instead. The blast kicked up more dirt. Rain did come later. Thornton said, "I'm glad [the towns] got moisture. And, if I had anything to do with it, I'm doubly glad."

Vocabulary

stoop (STOOP) to bend over

fertile (FUR-tuhl) capable of growing

shantytown (SHAN-tee-toun) an area with poorly built houses

ditch (DICH) a long, narrow hole in the ground

FLASH FACT!
Shantytowns sprang up all over the country in the 1930s.

27

FLORENCE: The government needs to build better migrant camps.

EVELYN: I just want a clean and safe space. At least I've made some friends. Other migrants are nice. But the **locals** won't even talk to us. When they do, it's to make fun. They think my **accent** is funny. They look at me like I'm trash.

DOROTHEA: Our country is in a **Great Depression**. Banks are failing. This means there aren't enough jobs for everyone. People think migrants are stealing their jobs.

FLORENCE: But things are changing. Dorothea and I hope our photos will help.

DOROTHEA: President Franklin Roosevelt has a lot of ideas. He's giving people jobs. He's helping farmers.

EVELYN: Things will get better. There's always a light in the storm.

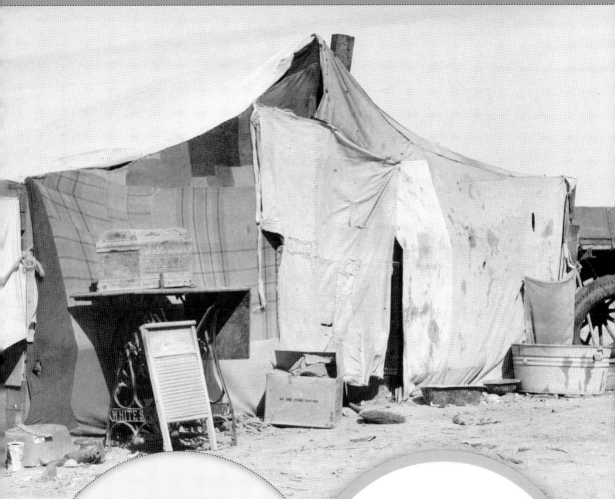

Vocabulary

locals (LOH-kuhlz) people who live in an area

accent (AK-sent) the way someone talks

Great Depression (GRAYT dih-PRESH-uhn) a period of time when the country's economy was in a slump

FLASH FACT!
Migrant worker camps were filled with homemade shelters. People used tents, tarps, and cardboard.

EVENT TIMELINE

May 20, 1862: President Abraham Lincoln signs the Homestead Act. The U.S. government gives free land to farmers. Other laws are passed. These laws encourage people to develop land in the West.

1910s and 1920s: World War I takes place. It increases Europe's demand for wheat. Farms struggle to keep up. They tear up grasslands to make more room for farmland.

1931: A severe drought hits the Great Plains. Crops die. "Black blizzards" begin. Dust from the overdeveloped land begins to blow.

1932: Dust storms increase. Fourteen dust storms are reported.

1933: There are 38 dust storms reported. Franklin D. Roosevelt is president. He passes laws to help banks and farmers.

June 18, 1933: The first soil erosion camp is set up in Alabama. Its goal is to help heal and protect the land. By September, there will be 161 of these camps.

May 1934: Dust storms spread. Dust covers 75 percent of the country. It severely affects 27 states.

June, 1934: The government forms the Drought Relief Service (DRS) to help people. The DRS buys cattle from farmers. This helps farmers.

April 8, 1935: President Roosevelt creates the Works Progress Administratsion (WPA). The WPA gives jobs to 8.5 million people.

April 14, 1935: "Black Sunday" happens. This is the worst dust storm. It causes a lot of damage. The term Dust Bowl is used for the first time.

April 27, 1935: Laws are passed to improve farming.

March 1937: President Roosevelt's Shelterbelt Project begins. Over 200 million trees were planted across the Great Plains.

1939: In the fall, the rain comes. The drought finally ends.

CONSIDER THIS!

TAKE A POSITION! Some people think the government should help people. It should solve people's problems. Other people think the government should stay out of people's affairs. They think people should solve their own problems. How did the government help with the Dust Bowl? Do you think the government should have gotten involved? Why or why not? Argue your point with reasons and evidence.

SAY WHAT? Learn more about the Dust Bowl. Explain the causes. Explain the effects.

THINK ABOUT IT! Think about how the Dust Bowl affected different people. How were people's experiences of the Dust Bowl affected by their roles in society? How were poor people affected? How were rich people affected? How were people of color affected? How were women affected?

LEARN MORE

Brown, Don. *The Great American Dust Bowl*. Boston: Houghton Mifflin Harcourt, 2013.

Marrin, Albert. *Years of Dust: The Story of the Dust Bowl*. New York: Dutton Children's Books, 2009.

Russo, Kristin J. *Viewpoints on the Dust Bowl*. Ann Arbor, MI: Cherry Lake Publishing, 2018.

Zuchora-Walske, Christine. *The Dust Bowl*. Ann Arbor, MI: Cherry Lake Publishing, 2014.

INDEX

ABOUT THE AUTHOR

Dr. Virginia Loh-Hagan is an author, university professor, and former classroom teacher. She hates dusting and anything to do with cleaning. She loves bowls and anything to do with eating. She lives in San Diego with her very tall husband and very naughty dogs. To learn more about her, visit www.virginialoh.com.